D1285264

UNSOLVED MYSTERIES OF NATURE

by Heather L. Montgomery

Consultant:
Michelle Fournier, Interpretive Naturalist
Chippewa Nature Center
Midland, Michigan

Edge Books are published by Capstone Press,
1710 Roe Crest Drive, North Mankato, Minnesota 56003
www.capstonepub.com

Library of Congress Cataloging-in-Publication Data
Montgomery, Heather L.
  Unsolved mysteries of nature / by Heather L. Montgomery.
    pages cm.—(Edge books. Unsolved mystery files)
  Includes bibliographical references and index.
  Summary: "Describes unsolved mysteries of nature from around the world"—Provided
by publisher.
  ISBN 978-1-4914-4265-4 (library binding)
  ISBN 978-1-4914-4341-5 (paperback)
  ISBN 978-1-4914-4321-7 (eBook PDF)
  1. Natural history—Miscellanea—Juvenile literature. I. Title.
  QH48.M6184 2016
  508--dc23   2014044887

Editorial Credits
Alesha Sullivan, editor; Sarah Bennett, designer; Gina Kammer,
media researcher; Morgan Walters, production specialist

Photo Credits
Alamy: © Danita Delimont, 24; AP Photo: MINN. POLLUTION CONTROL AGENCY, 23;
Dreamstime: © Ryan Jorgensen, 7; Freshwaters Illustrated: Dave Herasimtschuk, cover; Getty
Images: David McNew, 17; Glow Images: Science Faction, 11; Newscom: Design Pics, 8, Robert
Harding/Lee Frost, 20; Shutterstock: Africa Studio, (background) 14, art_of_sun, 28, Calin Tatu,
(background) 4, Claire McAdams, (fog smoky background) throughout, Darios, 14, Kirsanov
Valeriy Vladimirovich, 5, Konstanttin, (scales background) 7, 8, Mark Heider, (Earth map)
throughout, MisterElements, (ink splatters) throughout, Nemeziya, (honeycomb background) 12,
orxy, 18, Perutskyi Petro, 13, Tracey Patterson, (background) 22, 24; Wikimedia: Joe Thomissen,
27, 28

Printed and bound in the USA.
082018   000881

Contents

Nature's Tricks

Imagine seeing fish raining from the sky or lightning that chases people. Tingles run up your spine. You shake your head, blink your eyes, and become suspicious. How can this be happening? Maybe it is just a trick. You want to **investigate**, but your heart pounds and your palms sweat. It might not be safe. If the rules of nature are being broken, what else might go wrong?

You wouldn't be the only one asking these questions. Some of the greatest minds on the planet have puzzled over these same mysteries. They look for clues to get answers. They propose **explanations**. Get ready to explore some of nature's most puzzling mysteries!

investigate—to gather facts in order to discover as much as possible about an event or a person

explanation—a statement made to clarify something and make it understandable

4

Falling Fish

All across our planet, fish have rained from the sky. When fish drop from the clouds, people can't believe their eyes. They call out to their friends to make sure they aren't seeing things. Then they start to worry. What else might rain down on their heads?

People question whether this event really happens. It seems like a **hoax**. But many times throughout history, people have reported bizarre things falling from the sky. The falling items are often fish but not always. Many of these strange happenings have occured in the United Kingdom. Minnows plopped down on people in Knighton, Wales in 2004. In Coventry, England, a storm of apples brought traffic to a halt in 2011. In Croydon, England, hundreds of dead frogs rained down in 1998.

hoax—a trick to make people believe something that is not true

Some Items Reported Falling from the Sky

Item	Location	Date
alligators	South Carolina, USA	1877
jellyfish	Frankston, Australia	1935
maggots	Acapulco, Mexico	1967
frogs	Croydon, England	1998
minnows	Knighton, Wales	2004
apples	Coventry, England	2011

Are Storms to Blame?

Scientists say strong winds from nearby storms may be to blame. The fish in Knighton were found just after a thunderstorm. The apples in Coventry fell on a day when storms were predicted. The frogs in Croydon fell during a rain shower. **Waterspouts**, which may develop when storms pass over water, can whip wind at 100 miles (161 kilometers) per hour. Is that enough power to suck things up into the sky?

Something Fishy

People wonder about this answer. First, it has not been proven that waterspouts are strong enough to pick up thousands of items. Second, the items are usually all the same thing. How could the wind choose what it picks up?

Will this mystery ever be solved? It is difficult to predict when and where the next bizarre rainfall of objects will happen. Without this information it is hard to collect **evidence**. And without good evidence, it may remain a mystery for a long time.

waterspout—a mass of spinning cloud-filled wind that stretches from a cloud to a body of water

evidence—information, items, and facts that help prove something is true or false

Death Valley's Sliding Stones

In Death Valley in the western United States, large stones sit at the end of long winding grooves in the desert sand. It is obvious that the stones have slid into place. How can this be possible? There are no footprints. There are no tire tracks. There are no signs that point to people. It is as if a ghost slid each stone across the desert floor.

Clues

Some say the wind is to blame. Is it strong enough? It might need some assistance. Let's examine the evidence. First, the rocks traveled in the same direction as the wind. The desert wind howls up to 90 miles (145 km) per hour in this environment. Second, it rains in this desert a few times a year. Although the temperature is usually boiling hot, occasionally it dips below freezing. A slippery surface caused by wind gusts and freezing rain may be the **culprit**.

Another culprit may be a **bacterium** that lives in the desert sand. When it rains the bacterium becomes wet and gets slimy. Maybe it makes the sand slippery. Then the rocks could glide and sail along the ground when the wind blows.

Recent Discovery

Using high-power cameras and tracking devices, scientists caught the rocks in motion in 2014. During rare instances of below-freezing temperatures, thin sheets of ice were blown by the wind and rammed into the rocks. Inch by inch the ice shoved the rocks downwind. Scientists will continue to collect evidence until they are sure that they have the answer.

culprit—the cause of a problem or defect

A swarming, buzzing beehive suddenly goes silent. The honeycomb, eggs, and newborn bees sit eerily still. The adult bees have vanished. Why would the bees leave their home? In the winter of 2005-2006, thousands and thousands of adult honeybees in the United States disappeared from their hives without a trace. There were no dead bees, no clues as to where the bees went, and no evidence that explained why they left. Not long after, reports of bee disappearances came pouring in from across North America and Europe.

Worse yet, bees are still disappearing. People are beginning to wonder if all of the bees will vanish. Many experts agree that there must be more than one cause for the vanishing bees. That makes it extra tricky to solve this mystery.

Give a Bee a Helping Hand

Do you enjoy crunchy almonds or sweet cherries? Without bees these foods would not exist. Bees **pollinate** these plants. Disappearing bees is a big deal, but you can make a difference:

- Plant flowers around your house.
- Buy food from farms that plant a variety of crops.
- Teach your family about bees' roles in the environment.

pollinate—to transfer pollen from plant to plant; pollination helps flowers make seeds

13

The Suspects

In the summer of 2012, a Harvard scientist fed bees in 12 different hives a certain **pesticide**. Later that winter, the bees abandoned their hives. Bees that were not fed the pesticide stayed in their homes. But before anyone points a finger, more hives need to be studied.

A **parasite** could also be at fault. Tiny parasites, such as Varroa mites, drink the blood of bees and spread viruses throughout colonies. But no one has proven that the parasites cause bee colonies to mysteriously vanish.

Bees need plenty of flowers to survive. With more people on the planet, there are more buildings and fewer flowers. Even on farms there may be only one crop for acres. Once that crop is done blooming, a bee might have to fly miles to find food. Lack of food definitely affects the number of bees that survive. Does it cause adult bees to vanish? We still don't know.

pesticide—a poisonous chemical used to kill pests, such as insects

parasite—an organism that lives on or in another organism in order to get nourishment or protection

Monsters from the Sea

A long-horned beast, a hairless creature, gooey gray blobs—dead animals creep up on beaches across the globe. What are these mystery monsters?

When an unknown animal washes up on shore, people get excited. Everyone has a guess. Maybe it is a new creature we have never seen before. Or perhaps it is an animal rarely seen by people, such as a giant squid. It can be fun to guess what kinds of animals these are and where they came from, but it's still puzzling how they got onto the beaches.

Case Closed?

Sometimes these mysteries turn out to be pretty easy to solve. When a snakelike body washed up on a beach in Scotland in 2011, people called it a monster. But a veterinarian imagined the missing parts. He knew it was just part of a baby whale. Slimy gray globs found in Chile in 2003? Only blubber—nothing that exciting.

A mysterious blob washed up on Newport Beach in California in 2005. The blob was actually a giant squid.

Other instances of washed-up animals remain a mystery. In 2008 a four-legged body came ashore in Montauk, New York. Some say it was a raccoon, others claim it was a dog, and still others say it was a fake object created to cause confusion. To this day the Montauk Monster remains a mystery to many. Each new dead creature that washes up is a mystery to be solved.

Africa's Barren Polka Dots

A dry grassland in Namibia, Africa, is dotted with bare orange circles. In a landscape usually covered in grass, these dead zones do not make sense. They are like a rash on the earth. Will they spread across the planet? What causes the mysterious circles? Scientists from across the globe have traveled to Southwestern Africa to try to clear up unanswered questions.

The Details

The circles are 7 to 39 feet (2.1 to 12 meters) across. No plants grow inside the circles. Just outside of the circles, however, grasses often grow three times taller than other grasses in the area. Do the barren circles have special growing powers?

Namibia's barren circles dot the landscape and remain a mystery.

Good Guesses

People claim that dragons, gods, or UFOs made the circles. Some say the circles are hoaxes. Scientists have other **hypotheses**.

Scientists wonder if a barren circle is the result of an underground war for water. They know that circles are most common where there is little rain. They found that the soil near the edge of a circle is even drier than in the center. These researchers propose that the grass on the edge sucks the circle dry.

One scientist found sand termites in every circle. Perhaps the termites eat the grass. However, others question that idea. How could the termites cause the spots to be in a circular shape?

Not many people want to shell out money to study dirt and grass. So it may be a while before this mystery gets solved.

hypothesis—a prediction that can be tested about how a scientific investigation or experiment will turn out

Tall grasses thrive in the deserted landscape just outside of the empty, orange circles.

Freaky Frogs

In August of 1995, a group of schoolchildren pulled deformed frogs out of Ney Pond in the northern United States. There weren't just one or two weird frogs. More than half of the frogs had missing legs, missing eyes, or extra hind legs.

After a newspaper story about the frogs was released, more reports came tumbling in. Odd frogs were popping up all over North America—in parts of Minnesota, Ohio, Texas, and in Ontario, Canada. What was going on?

The Problems

This mystery isn't simple to study. After the **deformities** were discovered, the frogs in Ney Pond vanished for the winter. Students found them under the ice in a nearby river. Because the frogs traveled during their life cycle, the scientists had to search for evidence in the pond, on land, and in the river. There were many things such as pollution in their environment that could have affected the frogs. It was impossible to study every one of them.

In a pond in Minnesota, frogs were found with extra hind legs or stumps in place of legs.

deformity—being twisted, bent, or disfigured

What's to Blame?

After 20 years scientists still have no explanation. Why? It's not a clean case with any of the possible suspects. Pollution might be the cause. Frogs can take in water and air through their skin. That means they also soak up chemicals from the water. In a laboratory, when scientists grew tadpoles in polluted water, the tadpoles were damaged. Did chemicals in Ney Pond cause the deformities?

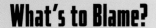

Other experts believe that a parasite living inside the tadpoles caused the frogs' legs to grow incorrectly. Laboratory tests were conducted. The deformities caused by that parasite did not match the deformities found in frogs living in Ney Pond.

It is possible that more than one factor caused the frog deformities. But we still don't have an answer.

An American bullfrog was discovered in the US with six legs. Scientists aren't sure what causes the deformities.

Balls of Lightning

A ball of lightning floats above the ground. It zigs, it zags, and then it heads straight toward you. Poof! It disappears. Ball lightning is bizarre. Normal lightning doesn't float across the ground. It doesn't act intelligent. And it doesn't chase people. Ball lightning does. Once it even bounced on a teacher's head—20 times! What's even more bizarre is no one knows exactly what it is or what's in it.

What We Think We Know

Ball lightning can be as small as a marble or as big as a car. Often it is the size of a softball. Ball lightning is usually red, but it also can be white, blue, purple, or green. Ball lightning can bounce, climb, or blast through a wall. Often it floats silently.

Because the balls seem to know where they are going, some people claim they are intelligent and possibly are aliens from another galaxy. Others think they are mini **black holes** or explosions from secret military tests.

black hole—the area in space around a collapsed star whose gravity sucks in everything around it, even light

Sprites, Jets, and Elves

From high above the clouds, astronauts have gotten great views of other spooky forms of lightning. Scientists classify odd lightning into different types:

Red Sprites: red or green flashes that are shaped like jellyfish and seen high above storm clouds

Blue Jets: bright blue cones of light, stretching about 25 miles (40 km) up from a cloud top

Elves: flat, glowing lights that last merely a millisecond yet swell up to 200 miles (320 km) across

People spotted an incredible ball of lightning in the Netherlands in 2011.

Making Lightning

Scientists have tried to reconstruct models of lightning to help answer their questions. With salt water, electricity, and a clay tube, experts in Berlin, Germany, created a floating, glowing ball of **plasma**. Did they create ball lightning?

Plasma clouds, which are similar to ball lightning, were created in a laboratory in Germany in 2006.

One researcher thinks ball lightning is made of **silica**. He proposed that regular lightning hits the ground and **vaporizes** silica. The chemical then rises as a ball and burns. But other scientists say this can't be the full story. They have watched lightning hit the ground hundreds of times and have never seen ball lightning.

Any Answers?

If the experts can't agree, will we ever know what ball lightning is? Some of the brightest minds on Earth are still burning to find answers.

Still Searching

The mysteries of nature are like puzzles. Finding solutions requires careful searching, seeking out hidden evidence, and proving an explanation. For many of these mysteries, people have found clues and made hypotheses. Yet experts are still looking for solid answers.

Why do fish fall from the sky? What strange creatures are crawling out of the sea? Can ball lightning really chase a person? Maybe someday you could be involved in solving one of these strange mysteries!

plasma—a highly charged state of matter that is usually formed only inside stars

silica—a chemical found in sand

vaporize—to be converted into vapor or fine particles of mist, steam, or smoke that can be seen hanging in the air

Glossary

bacterium (bak-TEER-ee-um)—a single-celled microscopic creature that exists everywhere in nature

black hole (BLAK HOHL)—the area in space around a collapsed star whose gravity sucks in everything around it, even light

culprit (KUHL-prit)—the cause of a problem or defect

deformity (di-FORM-it-ee)—being twisted, bent, or disfigured

evidence (E-vuh-duhnts)—information, items, and facts that help prove something is true or false

explanation (ek-spluh-NAY-shuhn)—a statement made to clarify something and make it understandable

hoax (HOHKS)—a trick to make people believe something that is not true

hypothesis (hye-POTH-uh-siss)—a prediction that can be tested about how a scientific investigation or experiment will turn out

investigate (in-VESS-tuh-gate)—to gather facts in order to discover as much as possible about an event or a person

parasite (PAIR-uh-site)—an organism that lives on or in another organism in order to get nourishment or protection

pesticide (PESS-tuh-side)—a poisonous chemical used to kill pests, such as insects

plasma (PLAZ-muh)—a highly charged state of matter that is usually formed only inside stars

pollinate (pol-uh-NAYT)—to transfer pollen from plant to plant; pollination helps flowers make seeds

silica (SIL-uh-kah)—a chemical found in sand

waterspout (WAW-tur-spowt)—a mass of spinning cloud-filled wind that stretches from a cloud to a body of water

vaporize (VAY-puh-rize)—to be converted into vapor or fine particles of mist, steam, or smoke that can be seen hanging in the air

Read More

Bingham, Jane. *Crop Circles.* Solving Mysteries With Science. Chicago: Capstone Raintree, 2013.

Doyle, James. *Young Scientists' Guide to Faulty Freaks of Nature: Including 20 Experiments for the Sink, Bathtub, and Backyard.* Layton, Utah: Gibbs Smith, 2013.

Simon, Seymour. *Strange Mysteries from Around the World.* Mineola, N.Y.: Dover Publications, 2012.

Internet Sites

FactHound offers a safe, fun way to find Internet sites related to this book. All of the sites on FactHound have been researched by our staff.

Here's all you do:

Visit *www.facthound.com*

Type in this code: 9781491442654

Check out projects, games and lots more at
www.capstonekids.com

Index